WONDER ABOUT THE PROPHET

I Wonder About the Prophet

Published by
THE ISLAMIC FOUNDATION

Distributed by
KUBE PUBLISHING LTD
Tel +44 (01530) 249230, Fax +44 (01530) 249656
E-mail: info@kubepublishing.com
Website: www.kubepublishing.com

First published in Turkey by Uğurböceği Publications,
a Zafer Publication Group imprint, in 2008.
This edition first published in 2016.

Author Özkan Öze
Translator Selma Aydüz
Series Editor Dr Salim Aydüz
Illustrator Sevgi İçigen
Book design Zafer Publishing & Nasir Cadir
Cover Design Fatima Jamadar

A Cataloguing-in-Publication Data record for this book is available
from the British Library

ISBN 978-0-86037-508-1
eISBN 978-0-86037-558-6

Printed by Imak Ofset, Istanbul, Turkey

BOOK

Özkan Öze

Translated by Selma Aydüz

Illustrations: Sevgi İçigen

The Prophet Muhammad does not appear in any of the pictures in this book.

Contents

Foreword

THE STORY OF the "I Wonder About Islam" series started one day with my son asking me, "Why can't I see Allah, dad?" The question was so unexpected that I didn't know what to say, although I actually knew the answer.

But when he asked so suddenly, I just said, "Umm, well…" He opened his eyes wide and started staring at me as if to say *Come on, give me the answer!* I beat around the bush for a while. You know, I was humming and hawing. In the end, I said, "Your eyes are so small, yet Allah is so big! This is the answer to the question. Because of this, you can't see Allah!"

"Oh, really?" he said. He turned his Spider-Man toy around in his hands. Then, as if he hadn't said anything, he went to his room. He was only five years old…

Perhaps, for a child his age, this answer was enough. I had handled the situation. However, as he got older, he would ask heaps of new questions about Allah. I had to prepare my answers.

So, that is how I started the "I Wonder About Islam" series.

The best thing about this book is that not only my kids, but kids from around the world can read my answers.

The first and second books in the "I Wonder About Islam" series consist of answers I have given to questions about Allah.

In the third book, you will find answers to questions about the Prophet, peace be upon him.

The fourth book is about the Muslim holy book, The Qur'an.

As for the fifth book, the topic is death and life after death. In particular, you will find answers to questions about heaven.

In the sixth book, I answer questions about belief in fate.

The last book of the series is about angels.

Have I answered all the questions about all these topics? Of course not! I've only tried to answer the most frequently asked ones. But if you look at how I have answered these questions, it will help you work out the answers to other questions yourself. If you hang on to your question's tail and pull as hard as you can, a huge answer will follow.

And after reading this book, you will see that questions don't frighten you as much as before. You will bravely ask the questions you thought were the hardest to answer, and soon you will see that you can't think of a question that doesn't have an answer. Asking a question is saying, "I want to learn!", "I want to understand!", "I want to know better and love more!" You should never be afraid of asking questions, and don't ever give up asking questions! Because a question is a key. Every question opens a door for you. And behind every door is a whole other world.

Furthermore, asking a question is also a prayer. Make sure you pray a lot so that your mind and heart are filled with the light of knowledge; so that your path is always bright.

The "I Wonder About Islam" series has been written using the works of the great Muslim scholar Said Nursi (1878–1960). The answers given to the questions and the examples to help you understand the topics have all been taken from his *Risale-i Nur* books.

Özkan Öze
İstanbul, 2012

A Messenger has come to you from among yourselves. Your suffering distresses him: he is deeply concerned for you and full of kindness and mercy towards the believers.

Surah Tawbah 9:128

Why do we need prophets?

WHEN WE WERE born we opened our eyes and found ourselves in a magnificent world. Just like a baby girl who wakes up in a room full of all the things that she needs, whatever we needed had been prepared for us in this magnificent world.

The sun was in the sky, brightening our day and also warming up this earth as if it was both a light and a heater.

When night came, the moon appeared like a comforting lamp and billions of stars were smiling like pearls in the heavens.

The calming colour blue was spread across the sky and the high seas, which were full of thousands of different types of fish…

Trees grew from the soil under our feet
and from their branches sweet cherries, pears,
oranges and other hundreds of different types
of fruit were extended toward us.

Just so we could drink sweet, nutritious
and warm delicious milk, great big cows were
grazing in lush meadows all day.

A tiny bee was living its life going from
flower to flower to make more honey than it
needed.

Clearly, we humans were taken care of.

Well, why was everything revolving around
us in such a way?

Who were we, for God's sake?

What business did we have here?

Where did we come to the earth from?

Why did the One who brought us here
bring us?

Were we just to sit among so many treats, so
many blessings, so much kindness?

Why did we have to leave this place of
beauty after living for some time on this earth?

These were big questions. We had to find answers to them.

Chosen teachers

We were like tiny sparrows lost in a thick forest of questions. The forest was so great and we were so small…

However, in this forest even ants had an advisor, bees a queen, a flight of swallows a head, the wild wolves a pack leader…

Were we going to be the only ones left leaderless?

Was Allah, who sent us to such a beautiful world, who created us so beautifully going to leave us without a guide?

Of course not!

Allah chose messengers from amongst us.

He spoke to them on behalf of all of us.

He informed them of the answers to our questions.

Why He created this world. This moon, this sun, these stars, the Milky Way… the blue planet, everything on the ground and in the heavens…

He let those messengers know why He created birds, fish, lions, tigers, bees, ants… and humans.

Why He sent us to this earth…

Where we are going from here…

And how we need to live here, what we need to do and stay away from as well…

So the messengers chosen from amongst us found out the answers to all of these questions and gave us lessons.

We call those chosen teachers PROPHETS.

For centuries, Allah chose many messengers from amongst us. They invited people to what is good and beautiful with their words, their lifestyles, with verses and books revealed to them.

Some of them had many followers. Everyone turned their backs on others.

They carried out every task Allah gave them.

Many of them were tortured. Many of them were exiled. Some amongst them were killed.

Allah sent new Prophets to fill the void of those who left the world after their tasks were over.

Adam, Enoch, Noah, Abraham, Isaac, Jacob and Joseph, Job, Moses and Aaron, David, Solomon and Jesus… were only some of the messengers chosen amongst us.

They were such good servants.

For humans, they were such beneficial teachers.

Centuries came and passed. Allah sent many other prophets. This continued until the last Prophet Muhammad Mustafa (peace be upon him).

He was the last messenger sent to humankind!

Why was the Prophet born in Makkah?

MORE THAN FIVE centuries had passed since Jesus left the earth. Time had trickled by and people had forgotten what God had revealed.

Truths that Jesus and other prophets before him had told, messages they had given, lessons they had taught… all were buried in the past.

No one cared why this world had been created…

Why were these flowers so beautiful?

Why were these fruits so delicious?

Why were the wings of these butterflies so decorative?

And why was this navy blanket that covered us up at night embellished with stars?

What was the flowing water saying? What about the voice of the wind?

The world needed a new teacher!

Humans had forgotten their humanity, along with many other things.

It had disappeared into a well as deep as the ocean, as dark as the night.

What fell in there first were justice, truthfulness, mercy…

Yes, the world needed a new teacher, a new prophet.

A prophet who was going to remind humans all they had forgotten; answer all questions; clean their hearts.

Why Makkah?

They say the darker the night is, the lighter the morning will be. In the year 571, the sun finally rose in Makkah.

The last Prophet was born.

You may ask the question, "Why Makkah?"

You may wonder, "Why was the Prophet born in the desert, in a small city?"

It is true that Makkah was just like an ordinary city in the Arabian Peninsula. Situated in a warm, dry, infertile valley, unsuitable for farming and unpleasant to the eyes.

But it had a feature different from all the other cities in the world:

THE KA'BAH!

The mother of cities

The Ka'bah, the first house of worship made for God, was in Makkah. For this reason, Makkah was considered the mother of cities. Allah mentions Makkah in the holy Qur'an:

This is a blessed Scripture that We have sent down to confirm what came before it and for you to warn the Mother of Cities and all around it.
                                    Surah Al-An'am 6:92

The Ka'bah was made by Adam, the first human and first prophet. Over time it had collapsed and been lost. However, Allah ordered Prophet Abraham to rebuild it.

Long centuries came and went and the Ka'bah became an important site throughout Arabia.

However, the Ka'bah, 'Allah's house' (Baitullah), became 'the house of idols' instead!

At the time of the Prophet Muhammad the people of Makkah knew of Allah's existence but they put large and small idols made out of wood, stone, clay, and soil between themselves and Him.

They asked for things they needed from the idols that they made with their own hands. Not directly from Allah

When they were scared, they would seek refuge in their idols, not in Allah.

When they set out on a journey, they would take the idols they had made out of halva (a sweet) with them and, when they got hungry, they would eat the idols that they had worshipped shortly before.

Supposedly, the idols drew them closer to Allah. Yet what they were doing was distancing themselves from Him.

The people who filled the Ka'bah with idols had hearts as dry as the desert and as hard as stone.

Their fathers buried their daughters alive in the earth.

Known or unknown, every type of corruption was an ordinary thing…

This was the place where the night of ignorance was darkest.

And the brightest sun since the creation of the earth was going to rise in this dark place; and shortly after it had risen, was going to astonish the whole world.

The sun that rose in Makkah

Since Prophet Adam, the Ka'bah has been was the place to worship Allah alone as God, asking only Him for the things we need, seeking refuge in Him alone when we're scared and only being scared of Him.

Which is why if a cleaning up of idols was going to take place on earth, this had to start with the Ka'bah in Makkah.

The flag rises from where it falls.

Makkah was the mother of cities.

Allah's house, the Ka'bah was there.

When the Prophet reached the age of forty, Allah sent the Angel Gabriel to him. Thus, his mission as a prophet began. The verses of the Qur'an were revealed to him for exactly twenty-three years.

During these twenty-three years, the Prophet, with the help of Allah, did many great things that weren't granted to anyone else in the history of the world.

The Ka'bah was cleaned of idols. Just as in the day of Prophet Abraham, Allah's masjid was on earth again.

However, before the Ka'bah, people's hearts and minds were cleaned of idols.

From those stone hearts, fountains of faith flowed after the Prophet's one look, one word, and one touch.

Those chests as dry and dusty as the desert turned into gardens with beds of roses.

The people abandoned all bad habits with his one word.

These were great things!

You see how much effort goes into making people give up a small habit such as smoking despite the danger to their health, but they remain unsuccessful!

The Prophet didn't stop at making them leave their bad habits but also replaced them with good ones.

Those people that buried their daughters alive were now being careful not to kiss their sons more than their daughters. Because the

Prophet amongst them told people to be fair, even when it came to kissing their children.

They threw away the jars of alcohol that they were drinking when they heard the order, "Allah banned it!"

Instead of taking someone's belongings against their will, they gave their own belongings to the poor.

The hungry were fed, the naked were clothed.

A bridge of brotherhood was being formed between the rich and the poor.

Ordinary people in the streets of Makkah and Madinah turned into stars.

Those stars were the friends of the Prophet.

We call them the companions.

The sun that rose in the mother of cities, Makkah, enlightened their hearts first.

Then this light dazzled the whole world's eyes...

What was Muhammad like before he was a prophet?

MUHAMMAD IBN ABDULLAH lived a normal life before he became a prophet, in a community where evil, cruelty and misery could be seen wherever one looked. However, his was a life as clean and pure as a drop of rain.

No evil touched him. No curse came near him. No drop of alcohol reached his throat or any impurity touched his flesh.

He led a clean, pure, true life.

The people of Makkah gave him the name AL-AMIN (trustworthy) because everyone trusted the Prophet.

His Lord was protecting him

During his childhood the Prophet was a shepherd. One day, alongside one of his friends, Muhammad was grazing his uncle's sheep somewhere near the city of Makkah. In the city of Makkah, there were entertainments in the evening. Men would gather people around them and tell them stories from the past. Our Prophet said to his friend:

"Could you look after the sheep while I go and watch?"

His friend agreed to this request and the Prophet started his journey towards Makkah. When he got close to the city, the sound of instruments and people shouting could be heard. It was a wedding party.

The Prophet sat at the side to watch the wedding. But as soon as he sat down a deep sleep came over him. He fell asleep right there. He didn't wake up until it was morning and the sun rose.

Another day he went towards the entertainers again hoping to watch an amusement. But again he was caught up in a deep sleep where he sat. After these two incidents, he never mixed with the indecent crowds again. He stayed away from their bad habits.

Avoiding idols!

As the Prophet stayed away from the evils of indecency, he also stayed away from idols.

Whether in his childhood, his youth or the years before he became a prophet, he never ever respected the idols.

He never bowed down in front of them, he never looked at them in admiration. He never believed in idols.

One day during his childhood, his uncle and his aunty wanted to take him to an idol during a celebration where offerings were made.

He said "I won't go!"

They got angry saying, "You're being disrespectful to our gods!" He accepted out of obligation. But when they got close to the idols the Prophet suddenly got lost. They looked but they couldn't find him. They searched and found him crouching in a corner, trembling with fear.

They asked him, "What happened to you?"

The Prophet answered:

"A man dressed in white came between me and the idol. And he told me to stay away from it!"

The Prophet never went anywhere near idols after this incident, and never put a hand on them or believed in them.

The Hanifs (Monotheists)

Before Islam, some people kept their distance from the idols, didn't believe in the idols and didn't bow down in front of them. They were the HANIFs.

Hanifs believed in Allah not the idols. They were the last representatives of the religion left from Prophet Abraham.

Although time had made people forget many things, the Hanifs believed in the oneness of Allah because of what they had heard from their grandfathers.

They saw worshipping, fearing and asking for help from idols made out of wood, stone and even sweets as a degrading thing.

They believed that Allah was going to send humans a new prophet and they were waiting

longingly for this prophet.

Some of them preferred to live alone to stay away from the darkness their people had fallen into.

Some sources say that the Prophet worshipped Allah as he heard and saw from the Hanifs. Even if it wasn't exactly like that, the Prophet's lifestyle was like the Hanifs' lifestyle anyway. Apart from the Hanifs in Makkah, there was also the Prophet who didn't believe in idols.

How did he pray?

During the last few years, before he was given the duty of prophethood, the Prophet would spend time alone. He wouldn't stay amongst people. He had found a cave for himself in a mountain near Makkah.

He came to this place called the cave of Hira very often. There he would turn towards his Lord and think only of Him.

Maybe he prayed in the way he saw and heard from the Hanifs or in the way Allah, who never left him alone, inspired him to do.

He would take some food with him that his wife Khadija had prepared and he would spend a few days in that lonely cave with his Lord.

This situation continued until one day the Angel of Revelation, Gabriel, came unexpectedly…

You yourself could not have expected the Scripture to be sent to you; it came only as a mercy from your Lord.

Surah Al-Qasas 28:86

Who named the Prophet?

TRY TO IMAGINE the days when Aminah was pregnant with the Prophet. Her pregnancy was going well. She didn't go through any of the difficulties pregnant women felt.

The only pain she felt was knowing that her baby was going to be born as an orphan because the Prophet's father had died months before he would be born.

A short time before the blessed birth, Aminah had a dream. In her dream she was directed to name her child 'Muhammad' and was told:

"You are pregnant with the most favoured of people… When he is born call him Muhammad!"

The day that the earth and the heavens had been waiting for finally came. Prophet Muhammad (peace be upon him) honoured the world.

Aminah told our Prophet's grandfather, Abdul Muttalib, of the amazing dream she had.

Seven days after our Prophet's birth, the happy grandfather took his blessed grandson in his arms and took him to the Ka'bah. He prayed there. He sacrificed animals and gave the meat to the poor. He fed the people of Makkah three times.

During one of those feasts, a dignitary of Makkah asked Abdul Muttalib:

"O Abdul Muttalib, what name did you give your grandson, that you've held feasts and given out treats to us because he was born?"

Abdul Muttalib said:

"I gave him the name Muhammad!"

This wasn't a commonly used name amongst them.

They found this name odd and asked:

"Why didn't you give him the name of someone in the family, or one of your ancestors' names? Why did you give him this name?"

The happy grandfather gave them this answer:

"I wanted Allah in the heavens and people on earth to praise him!"

After all, the name "Muhammad" means he who is worthy of praise.

The Prophet's beautiful names

The Prophet has many names. Some of these are in the Qur'an, some are given to him due to his unique characteristics.

I would like to tell you some of them and their meanings.

AHMAD: The most commendable

TAHIR: The pure

RASUL: The messenger

NASIR: The helper

BASHIR: The messenger of good news

SIRAJ: The lamp

AMIN: The trustworthy

JAWAD: The generous

UMMI: The unlettered

RA'UF: The kind

MUSTAFA: The chosen one

RASHID: The guide

MATIN: The strong one

MUNIR: The illuminating one

The Prophet has many names like these. Each is as beautiful as the other.

What is the Salawat?

WHEN LISTENING TO a talk about the Prophet, you must have heard Muslims say, "*Sallalahu alaihi wa sallam*" when the Prophet's name is mentioned. It means 'peace and blessings be upon him'.

This is called *salawat*.

Those who say the Prophet's name or hear it say salawat.

And in books where the Prophet is mentioned (pbuh) or (saw) is written so the reader remembers to say the salawat.

When I was small I didn't know the meaning of salawat and I just thought it was a mark of respect. Like 'the Great,' 'the Precious'…

However, much later I learned that salawat had a different meaning.

Before anything else, salawat was a prayer.

The word *salaat* had the meaning of prayer and mercy. And salawat is the plural of salaat.

By saying salawat when the Prophet's name is mentioned we pray for him; we ask for mercy from God for the Prophet.

"Allah!" we'll say, "let your mercy and blessing always be upon the Prophet."

It's not in our hands to give him a gift worthy of him. Please Allah you give it to him!"

Salawat is such a prayer.

Why is salawat so important?

Every salawat that rises from our tongue shows our love, attachment and loyalty to the Prophet Muhammad.

This is why salawat is so important.

Saying salawat every time we hear or read the Prophet's name is saying, "We didn't forget, O Allah's Messenger!

"We didn't forget the difficulties you faced when you brought Islam to the world, and the faith you taught us.

"Every time we hear your name, we say salaam and salat to you. We are your community, our commitment is to you!

"Every time we hear your name, we remember how much we love you and with every salawat we show our love.

"We push away all the centuries between us, and imagine you are still with us because we love you the most!"

Will the Prophet hear our salawats?

Wherever we may be, at whatever time of day when we say salawat, the words reach the Prophet. So does the name of the one who said it.

In one of his hadiths, the Prophet says:

"Send blessings upon me for your greeting will reach me no matter where you are."

– Abu Dawud

This is one of the best and most advantageous parts of saying salawat. Just think! You say one salawat to the Prophet, and with Allah's consent, it is reported to him straight away. Our Prophet accepts your salaam. In this way, you have greeted him!

Then what are we waiting for! Let's say a salawat:

Allahumma salli 'ala Muhammad wa 'ala ali Muhammad
(O Allah, bless Muhammad and the followers of Muhammad.)

Did the Prophet know how to read and write?

ONE OF THE characteristics of the Prophet was that he was 'illiterate'. Do you know what 'illiterate' means?

It means one who doesn't know how to read and write.

The opposite, somebody who is literate, is able to read and write, just like you.

Now let's come to our first questions:

Yes, but why was our Prophet illiterate?

Why didn't he know how to read and write?

Wouldn't it have been better if he had?

Illiterate (Ummi)

Before the duty of prophecy was given to the Prophet, the number of people who knew how to read and write in Makkah was about twenty-five. Being literate was an important privilege at the time of the Prophet.

Our Prophet did not have this privilege amongst people. Everyone knew he was illiterate.

For this reason, after the revelations started to come to the Prophet, the idol worshippers that he read the Qur'an verses to said many things to contradict him.

God forbid, they called him a "liar". God forbid, they called him a "Magician". God forbid, they said, "He must be crazy"…

They insulted him in many ways but since they knew quite well that he was illiterate they never said, "you read this from the Christians' and the Jews' books and learned it from there."

This also meant that nobody could raise these types of suspicions against the Qur'an.

Look how our Lord explains this mystery in the Qur'an:

You never recited any Scripture before We revealed this one to you; you never wrote one down with your hand. If you had done so, those who follow falsehood might have had cause to doubt.

Al-'Ankabut 29:48

As the Prophet was illiterate before he was a prophet, he stayed illiterate after as well.

Revelations came to him for exactly twenty-three years. So how were the Qur'an and his actions recorded? By scribes. Especially after he migrated to Madinah.

In Madinah more than 50 scribes were employed to write down the revelations. The companions who knew how to read and write were always with the Prophet.

They wrote down the verses brought by Angel Gabriel, right by his side, as soon as they were revealed. Then they made copies of what they wrote.

The reading and writing were not limited to this. The Prophet made them write the letters he sent to the kings of distant countries, and made them read the letters that arrived.

When our Prophet arrived in Madinah, the number of people who could read and write amongst the people of Medina was about ten. This number multiplied around him.

In such an environment with so many people learning how to read and write, of course the Prophet could have learned.

Yet, he never learned.

Those who wanted to question the verses of the Qur'an and the Prophet never had this chance, this door always remained closed.

Illiterate but still a Prophet

Allah did not allow His Messenger to be someone's student. He never allowed him to kneel before someone else, learn how to read and write from someone else.

The Prophet was illiterate but at the same time he was a prophet. What's more, he was the last Prophet. He was the last and highest of prophets.

It was no one's place to act as a master to him, and teach him something he didn't know…

Whatever he needed to know, Allah would let him know.

A person who gets news and verses from an

angel like Gabriel of course does not need to read something humans have written.

Therefore, this was the other reason the Prophet was illiterate…

He couldn't read the books humans wrote. He didn't need to. But there were two books that no one else could read, understand and explain to others better than he could.

One of the two books was the holy Qur'an. The other was this book of the universe, which when we open our eyes and look, is full of wisdom about the heavens and the earth and all its glory…

Let's open up the subject a bit more.

"Read!"

The duty of prophethood had not yet come to Muhammad. He regularly got away from crowds and lost himself in deep thoughts.

He spent days and nights all alone in the cave of Hira, on Mount Nur a few kilometres away from Makkah.

Towards the end of one of the nights the Prophet spent in the cave, Allah sent the Angel of Revelation, Gabriel, to him.

When the Prophet saw Angel Gabriel in front of him, he got scared. He couldn't understand what was happening.

Gabriel said:

"Read!"

The Prophet answered:

"I don't know how to read!"

Gabriel hugged the Prophet and squeezed him until he lost his breath. Then he said:

"Read!" again.

The prophet said:

"I don't know how to read!" again, with a shaky voice.

The Angel Gabriel hugged the Prophet tightly again. Then, he said:

"Read!" one more time.

The prophet said again:

"I don't know how to read." But as he saw that Angel Gabriel was not accepting this answer, he asked curiously:

"Tell me what I should read?"

After this question, Angel Gabriel started to read the first few verses from Surah Al-'Alaq in the Qur'an:

Read! In the name of your Lord Who created: He created man from a clinging form. Read! Your Lord is the Most Bountiful One who taught by the pen, Who taught man what he did not know.

Al-'Alaq 96:1-5

These are the first verses of the Qur'an that were revealed. And the revelation had started with the instruction to "Read!" to an illiterate prophet.

Well, let's think about this. Why does Allah order the Prophet, who couldn't read, to "read" in the first verse he reveals to him?

How was an illiterate Prophet going to read?

Unless it wasn't the 'reading' we knew of?

The first order of Islam: Read!

So about 1400 years ago, Allah ordered an illiterate person from a community that lived in ignorance, to READ!

Read! In the name of your Lord Who created: He created man from a clinging form. Read! Your Lord is the Most Bountiful One.

The Prophet did as he was asked. He read the Qur'an to people verse by verse for twenty-three years. He explained, taught, made them memorize… again and again… countless times.

And that illiterate Prophet read the book of the universe to people too.

He read the book of the universe explaining the pages from the stars, the clouds, the mountains, the lush meadows, the vast deserts, and the trees leaf by leaf, the flowers, the fruits, the vineyards, the gardens, the seas, the streams, the sweet cool fountains…

From the birds, the bees, the horses, the camels with humps, a thousand and one variety of fish and humans… and he taught us how to read "in the name of your Lord Who has created"…

With the lesson that we learned from him, we saw that whatever we look at is Allah's creation.

With every lesson that we learned from him we knew that Allah created every being from nothing.

With the lesson that we learned from him, we believed only in Allah and His oneness...

The Prophet, the greatest teacher, taught us like this. He had read like this, and taught us to read like this...

Why was a person chosen to deliver Allah's message?

THE PROPHET WAS one of us. He was a messenger chosen from amongst the people, for the people.

If, instead of a messenger, Allah had sent down an angel from the heavens that angel could not have been a teacher for us. We could not have taken its life as an example for ourselves.

Neither could it live like us; nor would we live like it!

Our lives wouldn't be similar. Our pain, our happiness, our fears, things we enjoy and things we don't, would be very different.

How could an angel or a strange human who doesn't get hungry, thirsty, or tired be a prophet to us ordinary people who get hungry, thirsty, and tired, who get cold in the cold and hot in the heat?

The head of ants is chosen from amongst ants.

The queen of bees is ultimately a bee.

Again, a swallow leads a flight of swallows.

The prophet of humankind should of course be a human.

Let us remember what the Prophet taught us with his life just about eating:

He said "bismillah" when he sat down to eat.

He ate with his right hand and ate from in front of him.

When he ate he didn't lean somewhere and reach out.

He didn't fill his stomach completely. He left the table before he was completely full.

After he finished eating, he thanked his Lord. He washed his hands.

He enjoyed crowded meals.

He gave feasts to his friends.

He accepted invitations from others. When he was going to those invitations, he got special permissions from the host for the people that joined him on the way.

He never complained about any food that was put in front of him.

When he couldn't find anything to eat he was patient, he fasted and sometimes he even tied a stone to his stomach so he didn't feel the hunger.

The Prophet was a prophet but at the same time was a human.

If we had a prophet who never felt hunger, or if an angel was sent to us as a prophet, could he have been such a good example to humans?

Would he have lived like us? Could he understand us? And could we live our lives in the way he lived his? Could we take him as an example to us? Could we carry out the advice he gave us? Could we do what he did?

And could we love him this much?

For example if an angel was sent to us as a prophet, I wonder how much we could love an angel.

I think we could only love him as much as the Angel of Revelation, Gabriel. Maybe a bit more.

But as it would still be an angel, and we are human, our love would be different.

Maybe it would be as different as a human loving rainbows on one hand and loving their father on the other!

The Prophet is one of us, a messenger chosen from amongst us…

He's a father above our father, dearer than our mother…

A strand of his hair is more precious than our life…

He is neither an angel nor someone who doesn't get hungry or thirsty…

He is one of us!

But at the same time, our Prophet!

He is a Prophet!

I think you understand the reason behind Allah choosing a messenger from amongst us. But there's a point I want to talk about.

When you read books about the Prophet, you will find very different examples of his human side.

At one point, you see that he's lifted his grandchildren on his back and is carrying them.

Then, he's playing around with kids in the streets of Madinah and entertaining them.

Another time, he's putting tar on the feet of his horse.

And another, he's fixing the shoes he wears on his blessed feet.

Another time, he's bargaining with a bedouin in the market.

All of these memories are as precious as treasures for us. Every moment of his unique life is a direct example to our own lives.

But if we only look at this human side of

the Prophet, we might make a mistake.

There may be some confusion in a tiny corner of our minds.

A whisper that disturbs us:

"So you see, he was an ordinary person too," it will try to say, "an ordinary person like you and me..."

We may forget that he's in an unreachable position…

I'm going to give you two important examples from a book about this topic I really love.

Think of a tree, a huge tree with branches that reach the Milky Way. Like every tree, it would have a seed. If you hold the seed in your hand and try to see all the characteristics of that huge tree, all the beauty, its branches, fruits and strong roots there, you won't see it! Because what's in your hands isn't a tree, it's just a seed.

If you look at the seed in your hand and say, "This is a simple piece of wood!" you would be mistaken.

If you want to see the tree, you must lift your head and look at that splendid tree with branches that reach the Milky Way.

Only in this way, can you see all the brilliance of this miraculous tree.

Now think of a peacock!

A magnificent peacock that has a tail of so many different colours…Then think of the egg that the peacock came from…

If you look at the egg, and try to see a magnificent peacock there, you won't see it!

You would say, "This ordinary egg has neither colour nor beauty!" You would be unfair to both the egg and the peacock.

Therefore, you must lift your head and look at that magnificent bird. You can only see its beauty in this way.

The Prophet's human lifestyle, eating like an ordinary person, getting tired, sitting with his friends, playing with kids is like the seed of that magnificent tree and the egg which that enchanting peacock came out of.

When you look at those things, and you hear the whisper that disturbs you saying, "Where is the master of the universe? Where is the Master of all prophets? Where is the dearest messenger of Allah, who created everything for him? I see an ordinary person!" immediately lift your head…

Lift your head and look!

Remember that he is a Prophet that billions of people mention every day, say salaam and salaat to!

Lift your head and look!

Recall that with the religion the Prophet brought, a community that would bury its children alive, in a short amount of time, became a fair and educated people!

Lift your head and look!

Think that he is the messenger of our Lord, who created the earth and the heavens and everything in between.

Lift your head and look!

Think of how for twenty-three years the Angel of Revelations, Gabriel, brought him the verses of Allah…

Don't look at how he joked around with children, fixed the shoes he wore on his blessed feet by his own hands, bargained in the market and be fooled!

Lift your head and look!

Remember how the Prophet went from Makkah to Jerusalem in one night, and from there went on the journey of Miraj that wasn't granted to any other person, any other prophet!

Only then, you may start to understand what kind of a prophet he was.

Did the Prophet Muhammad perform miracles?

THERE'S A BIG chance that people in the same class as me that day don't remember this. But I do...

I remember very well, almost twenty-five years ago, our Islamic school teacher said, "The only miracle our Prophet performed is reciting the Qur'an! He doesn't have any other miracles like the other prophets!"

In a strange way, I never forgot these words our teacher said.

For years this sentence came to my mind in the most unexpected places, at unexpected times. I thought about it a lot.

I guess knowing the other prophets had performed a variety of miracles but our Prophet having the Qur'an as his only miracle troubled me as a child.

Allah sometimes created miracles for the messengers he gave hard jobs to.

The fire that Nimrod had thrown Prophet Abraham into hadn't burned Prophet Abraham.

Prophet Jonah had lived in the stomach of the giant fish.

The staff in Prophet Moses' hands had turned into a snake in front of the pharaoh.

For Prophet Moses and his believers, Allah had split the Red Sea in half.

Feasts had come down from the sky for Prophet Jesus. Allah had cured the wounds of lepers through his hand, and even resurrected the dead with one touch.

The task of a prophet was a really hard job.

And sometimes Allah created such miracles for His prophets.

Then He must have created miracles for the Prophet Muhammad.

Of course, the Qur'an is the greatest miracle. It's a miracle that's still alive in front of our eyes today.

Yes, but why shouldn't our Prophet have performed any other miracles?

After many years, when I read a book about the Prophet's miracles I realised that my school teacher had, without knowing, given us wrong – or let's say incomplete – information.

The Prophet Muhammad had performed other miracles apart from revealing the Qur'an.

What is a miracle?

I was thinking of giving you some examples from the miracles in our Prophet's life now, but before that we need to answer the question, "What is a miracle?"

In short, everything that only Allah can do is a miracle.

You might think that in this way, everything is a miracle. For example, an apple growing on a tree branch is not something humans can do. Only Allah can do this. Therefore, an apple is a miracle.

Yes true!

However much a piece of wood turning into an apple is a miracle we have learned to expect it. But if Allah wants, a tree can even turn into a sword. That would be unexpected.

The example of a sword didn't randomly come to my mind.

Think back to the fiercest moments of the Battle of Badr, the first time the Prophet fought with the enemies.

The Muslim army was much smaller in number than the army from Makkah. Ukasha, one of the most glorious and brave soldiers of that small Muslim army, broke his sword.

In that moment, what Ukasha needed the most was a sword. But no one had an extra sword.

When the Prophet saw that Ukasha's sword broke, he gave him a stick and ordered: "Go fight with this!"

As soon as Ukasha took that stick, he threw himself onto the enemy.

And in that moment a miracle happened. Allah turned the stick in Ukasha's hand into a shining sword.

Ukasha used that miraculous sword in that battle, and also in all the other wars he fought in for Allah for the rest of his life.

Allah creates the miracles!

If heaps of questions come to your mind about
how a stick can be turned into a sword, don't
worry! This is completely normal. A piece
of wood turning into a metal sword is not
something any human can understand.

Because this is a miracle!

A miracle, in other words, is something that
leaves a person helpless! It is something only
Allah could do…

Wood turning into a wooden sword is hard
to understand but it could happen under some
circumstances.

For a piece of wood to turn into a metal
sword there's only one explanation:

Allah's wish!

If Allah wants, wood will turn into a sword
made of metal, and even into a snake like
Prophet Moses' staff…

As we said at the start; however impossible
these things are for us; wood becoming

an apple, a grape, an orange are equally impossible. All of these fruits in front of our eyes are not less of a miracle than Ukasha's sword.

You must look at the miracles Allah created for the prophets in the centuries before the Prophet Muhammad from this point of view.

Allah creates miracles, not humans – even if they are prophets. Don't forget this.

The Prophet's miracles

Allah created many miracles for the Prophet. If we tried to put all of the miracles from the Prophet's life into one book it would need to be thousands of pages long.

For that reason, I want to tell you only about the ones that have affected me the most, very briefly, in a few sentences.

One day, a man from the desert brought a big lizard to the Prophet and said:

"If this lizard accepts your prophethood, I will as well!"

Our Prophet asked the animal:

"Who am I?"

The lizard said, "You are Allah's messenger!" in a voice loud enough for everyone there to hear it.

Another day, a man from the desert came to the Prophet and said:

"Show me a miracle so that I believe in your prophethood!"

Our Prophet ordered the man from the desert:

"Say to that tree over there, Allah's Messenger is calling you!"

The man did as he was told and called out to the tree:

"O tree, Allah's Messenger is calling you!"

That tree lifted its roots from the soil with crackling noises, came to the Prophet and said:

"Greetings to you, o Allah's Messenger!"

It was the time of a military expedition. The Islamic army's water was about to run out. They told the Prophet that there wasn't enough water left to do wudu, the prescribed wash before prayer.

The Prophet ordered for the water to be collected.

A little drop of water was brought.

The Prophet prayed over the water. But no one heard how he prayed.

Then he ordered them to bring a large pot.

They brought a big vessel.

He put his blessed hands in the vessel and opened out his fingers. Then he ordered them to slowly pour the water on his hands.

They slowly started to pour the water onto the Prophet's hands.

Water started flowing from the Prophet's fingers like fountains. Everyone there saw this. That great vessel filled and overflowed. The thirsty drank water. Those who wanted to do wudu did it. Those who had waterbags filled them up. When the need for water was over, the Messenger of Allah lifted his hands out of the vessel. The vessel was still full of water.

The mother of the Prophet's small attendant Anas had made a little bit of food. She gave the food to Anas and asked him to give it to Allah's Messenger.

When the Prophet saw the food, he said to Anas:

"Invite him, him and him! Then invite whoever you see on the way to eat!"

The Prophet prayed over that small amount of food. Almost three hundred men came and ate from it. But the food didn't finish.

During the battle of Uhud, an arrow hit Qatada b. Numan's eyes. His eye came out of its socket and onto his cheek. When Allah's Messenger saw him like this, he put his eye back in its place with his blessed hands and prayed.

Qatada b. Numan's eye suddenly healed. It was even better than his other eye.

As the Prophet wasn't just the prophet of the

people he lived among like past prophets, so he also wasn't just the prophet of humans.

He is the prophet of humans, jinns, and all beings that filled the earth and heavens.

Allah created him to be a mercy to the universe. And everything recognised him and accepted his prophethood.

Before the duty of prophecy was given to him, the clouds made shade above him.

The angels revolved around him, trees and stones that saw him greeted him.

When they were on the migration journey, the spider in front of the cave near Makkah guarded him.

The wooden pillar that he rested his back on had started to cry like a camel and moan in front of the companions just because he left.

Tired camels knelt in front of him and complained about their troubles.

Those who came to him with a snake's sneakiness with the intention of killing him, fell in love with him with one look from him, one word one touch and one smile.

News about the future that came out of his blessed lips came true exactly as he had said years and years later.

During great droughts, when he opened out his hands to his Lord to ask for rain, rain was sent from the doors of heaven to rescue the dry soil and cracked lips, before he even put down his hands.

The wounds he touched with those blessed hands healed immediately.

Stones those hands held started to speak.

From the fingers of those hands, cool water flowed like it does from a mountain spring.

With one signal of that hand, the moon split.

Yes, that hand was the hand of Allah's Messenger.

A hand that performed many miracles, all created by Allah.

How did the Prophet treat animals?

THE PROPHET'S LOVE and compassion shone like the sun, illuminating and warming everyone and everything. Except the ones who turned their backs towards him with stubbornness, nothing, no being that breathed missed out on this.

The camels, horses, goats, cats, birds… everything, but everything, got their share of his love and compassion.

Before his time, during the period of ignorance, people treated animals very badly.

They used to sit on camels for hours and chat. They used the poor animals like couches

and never thought that they were alive and they could get tired.

They would cut the ears and tails of their animals, and burn their faces with hot irons so they wouldn't be mixed up with others' animals.

During long journeys, they would pierce their camels' bodies and drink their blood. They would even cut meat off live animals and then sew up the place they had cut it from.

They would do many other cruel things like this to animals without hesitation.

The Prophet banned torturing animals in this way, and even saying bad things to them and cursing them.

He liked horses and camels the most.

He ordered their maintenance and feeding to be done with care.

One day, he saw a camel that was moaning and crying.

The Prophet patted the poor animal's head and then found out who owned the camel.

The Prophet said to the owner of the camel:

"Have you no fear of Allah? Allah bestowed this animal upon you. But it has just complained to me that you leave it hungry and very tired!"

Sheep and goats were also animals the Prophet showed an interest in. He would see them as plenitude and called them "animals of heaven".

As I'm a sad cat lover, I used to wonder "What does our Prophet say about cats?"

It turns out, the Prophet liked cats as well!

If only you knew how happy I was the day I found this out.

One day when he was getting ready to do wudu, a cat came and started to drink from the water the Prophet was going to do wudu from. The Prophet waited until the cat had drunk the water, didn't scare it, and did wudu afterwards. Those who were there asked Allah's Messenger if the water got dirty?

The Prophet replied in this way:

"Cats are not dirty, they mingle with you."

One day he told his friends a story about a woman who went to hell, as she didn't give her cat food and water and caused the poor cat to die.

And another day, a man who gave a hot, thirsty dog a drink, by filling up his shoe with water had all his sins forgiven…

The Prophet also said to the ones who asked him, "Do we get a reward for good things we do to animals?"

He said, "Yes, there is a price for the good done!"

One day, he came across a very thin camel. His facial expression changed suddenly; he felt very sorry for that camel and warned the owner:

"Fear Allah when you look after this animal that can't talk!"

The Prophet was so sensitive about treating animals nicely that whenever he saw fault in this matter he would warn them.

One day he saw Aisha, his wife, who he loved more than anyone else, being a little harsh towards her camel and warned her:

"Mercy isn't shown to those who don't show mercy!"

The Prophet liked birds a lot, especially pigeons. He enjoyed watching them fly; he recommended those who complained of being lonely to keep pigeons.

I gave you a few examples of the great love and compassion the Prophet showed to animals during his beautiful life. I want to tell you one last one.

The Islamic army that set off to conquer Makkah was about ten thousand people. The Prophet marched at the front.

They suddenly saw a dog feeding its puppies. The mother had recently given birth.

The Prophet immediately put up a guard for them. This guard remained there until the whole army had passed. In this way the dog and her puppies didn't get trampled on, or feel uncomfortable.

This army, which wouldn't turn back from its journey for any reason, changed its path just so some puppies wouldn't get scared or harmed.

Did the Prophet like children?

THE PROPHET WIPED the tears of a tired camel in the streets of Madinah, its head and consoled it. Of course, he also loved children a lot.

He greeted children playing in the street and stroked their heads as well.

The kids surrounded him, and kissed his hands that smelled like roses on a cool morning.

He never made a distinction between boys and girls, who, at the time, were seen as inferior and often buried alive.

Once he came to the masjid with a small girl in his arms and prayed (salah) with that little girl.

And once he finished the prayer (salah) early because a child was crying.

He called his small attendant, Anas, 'My little one'. He loved him a lot. When he was naughty, he never got angry and always forgave him. He also never allowed anyone to get angry and insult him.

He never said, "Why did you do this like this?" or "Why didn't you do this" to Anas who served him for ten years.

He joked around with kids. He played games with them, raced with them, hugged them, embraced them, kissed them.

Whenever someone offered him fruit fresh from the branch, his sacred eyes would scan the area for a little child. Because the Prophet wanted children to eat the fresh fruit offered to him, before anyone else.

He would lift his darling grandchildren, Hasan and Husayn, on his back, and carry

them around like a camel walking about with
its travellers.

He ordered, "Those who have kids should
turn into kids with them".

To a group of desert men who said "we don't
kiss our kids" he said angrily:

"What can I do if Allah took the
compassion out of your hearts?"

It was the last hours of his journey from
Makkah to Madinah.

The people of Madinah had lined up on the
road to greet the Prophet.

When the Prophet got close to the city, he greeted the kids that were running towards him.

The kids were shouting:

"We love you! We love you!"

Our Prophet smiled at them with his face gleaming like the Sun and the Moon and said:

"I love you too!"

He even wiped the tears of tired camels in the streets of Madinah, petted their heads, and consoled them.

Of course, he also loved children and the children also loved him a lot.

Did the Prophet have fun and joke with his friends?

I UNDERSTAND WHY you hesitate to ask this question. You are someone who likes playing jokes on your friends. And now you wonder whether the Prophet played jokes on his friends?

I need to first tell you that our Prophet was not a grumpy person.

Compared to all of his closest friends, he was the one that smiled the most. But it was rare for him to laugh so much that his teeth showed.

When it comes to joking, yes the Prophet also played jokes on his friends from time

to time, made them smile and left beautiful memories in their hearts that would never be forgotten.

One day, one of his friends asked:

"O Allah's Messenger, do you joke around with us as well?"

The Prophet replied:

"Yes, but I never say something that isn't true!"

In this answer, he had given the measure of joking both to them and to all his future ummah.

Yes, from his lips – as even his enemies confessed – nothing but the truth would be told, even if it was a joke.

Now I'm going to give you a few examples from the jokes the Prophet played on his friends. Then you will be able to see what a joke is like without lying, cheating and of course harm!

One day, a man came to the Prophet and asked for a horse for himself.

The Prophet replied:

"Let's mount you on a female camel's child!"

The man was surprised: "O Allah's Prophet! What could I do with a female camel's child! That won't do my job!"

The Prophet replied to him with a smile:

"Aren't all camels the children of a female camel?"

Again, another day, one of the women companions came to the Prophet. She had questions to ask, and maybe a wish. Maybe she simply just wanted to see him.

At one point, the Prophet asked her:

"Aren't you the wife of the man with white in his eye?"

The woman was surprised:

"O Allah's Messenger, my husband doesn't have white in his eyes!" she said.

The Prophet replied with a smile:

"Everyone has white in their eyes!"

Another day an old woman came to see the Prophet.

"O Allah's Messenger!" she said, "Pray for me so I go to heaven."

The Prophet replied:

"Old women will not go to heaven!"

The woman was surprised, since the one talking was a prophet.

"Don't worry!" said the Prophet. "Don't worry! I mean, you will enter heaven not as an old woman but as an adolescent!"

The Prophet had set some limits to the jokes his friends played with each other. These limits apply to all Muslims for all time.

Do not lie even if it's a joke. Hiding someone's precious belongings or making jokes that scare people were not seen as pleasant by the Prophet.

You asked, and I explained. I hope you will be careful of the jokes you play from now on.

What is the Sunnah of the Prophet Muhammad?

A HEAD TEACHER is a head teacher on school grounds. When he leaves the school, for example goes shopping, he isn't a head teacher there. He would do his shopping not like a head teacher, but like any other person who has gone shopping that day.

No one ever wonders, "How does a head teacher do his shopping?" anyway.

A general is a general when he is in front of his army. He's not a general at his home. When he gets tired and goes to bed, he wouldn't lie down and sleep like a general but as an ordinary person.

No one needs to know how a general sleeps, which way he turns when he sleeps.

But a prophet is a prophet every second of his life.

Not only during the times revelations are given to him, or when he's calling out to others, inviting them to religion, to believe in Allah, calling them to abandon the idols; he's a prophet when he's shopping, and sleeping…

He's a prophet when eating a meal, when drinking water, when fighting in war, when meditating, when giving a talk, when smiling, and walking, when sitting with his wife at home, when praying (salah), when praying (dua), when fasting, he's always a prophet.

For this reason, whatever the Prophet did, he did as a prophet. He lived every moment of his life with a righteousness that befitted a prophet, and a beauty that's expected from one chosen to guide others. His life was free from wrongs and mistakes because Allah had taught him how to do everything.

The Prophet lived how Allah wanted him to. His lifestyle is the lifestyle Allah wanted to show.

The Sunnah is what needs to be taken as an example from the Prophet's flawless life, his state, his manner, things he recommended, things he did occasionally, things he never left out. For those who want to live a life Allah likes and approves of, Sunnah means both a shortcut and a bright and correct road.

If we have lived a life that matches the Prophet's Sunnah, we have lived a life that is similar to his.

It's just like if you love someone, you also like being like them; so Allah, as He loves the Prophet also likes those who try to be like him. Trying to be like him also means trying to match his sunnah. Each sunnah you copy is rewarded by Allah.

This is why 'The Prophet's Sunnah' is so important.

Reward machine

Keeping to the Prophet's Sunnah turns many ordinary jobs during the day into rewarding deeds.

For example when leaving the house the Prophet stepped out with his right foot first. If you did the same you would have kept to a sunnah. In this way, you would get a reward for following the Sunnah.

If you put on your right shoe first, you would have kept to another sunnah. For that, you will get another reward.

If you want I will give you some examples of sunnahs that will earn you lots of easy rewards:

- Smiling at your friends.
- Turning on to your right side when you go to bed (once you're asleep it doesn't matter which way you turn).
- Removing stones that might trip someone up or something that might block someone from a path.
- Planting a tree.
- Eating with your right hand (if there are no obstacles).

- Washing your hands before and after eating.
- Cleaning your mouth and teeth.

These are the ones that first come to mind. Of course, hadith books and books explaining the Prophet's life will have many other examples like these.

Whichever one you do, you will have acted like the Prophet, and done as he did. And those who copy the Prophet will earn rewards from Allah.

Sunnah makes life more beautiful

Does following the Prophet's Sunnah only earn us reward? Although that is enough, we also see the reward of trying to make our lives similar to the Prophet's on this earth.

Copying the Sunnah makes life more beautiful.

If we tried to live our lives like the Prophet, if we were making an effort to act in a manner that would suit his Sunnah, each more helpful than the other, we wouldn't be going through many of the problems we are going through today.

We would respect the elderly and love the young.

There wouldn't be tearful elderly people in retirement homes.

We would try to make children happy and race each other to care for and look after orphans.

Neighbours would look after each other and trust each other. No one would be able to sleep when their neighbours are hungry.

There would be bridges of kindness between the poor and the rich.

And all the workers' money would be paid before the sweat on their foreheads even dried.

You wouldn't see people with tangled hair and bad smells in the streets.

And many other goodnesses like these sunnahs from his beautiful life would shine on our lives like the sun.

"If the Prophet lived today would he clean his teeth with miswak (stick toothbrush) or with a toothbrush?"

TO ANSWER THIS question that most likely comes to mind as you brush your teeth in the morning, I have to remind you of two important points.

In the question you ask, "If our Prophet lived today…" But our Prophet isn't alive today. He is not with us anymore.

However much we want him to be amongst us, to see him, to sit by his side, to stroke our hair with his hands that smelled like roses on

a cool morning, to smile at us with the unique smile that brightens dark nights…however much we miss him, the Prophet, the dearest person to our hearts, doesn't live amongst us anymore…

Therefore answers given to questions that start with "If our Prophet lived today…" should start with, "Our Prophet doesn't live amongst us today."

Because if our Prophet lived amongst us, the world wouldn't be as it is. It would be completely different. Without doubt it would be a much more beautiful world.

The century we're living in would be 'the era of bliss'. And in this kind of world, you wouldn't be asking such a question anyway. Because you would know the answer!

Just like when we read about the lives of the companions and say, "Oh if only I was there with them!" you would see how the Prophet lived, how he did things. And you would try to live as you saw have live.

I also need to remind you of this:

As you know, younger people go to the elders. They visit them. The elders don't go to the younger people.

Therefore, it's not right to bring the Prophet to today but to take ourselves to the Era of Bliss and learn how the Prophet did things from books that explain his life.

In short, instead of, "How would our Prophet do something if he lived today?" we should say, "How did our Prophet do something?" This would be a more correct question.

I can't answer a question that starts with "If our Prophet lived today..." because I can't speak on his behalf.

Also there wouldn't be an end to such questions. If you answer one, another will come along. Such as, "So, would he go to football? Would he support a team? If he did what team would he support?"

As I said before what is right and is our duty is to find out how the Prophet lived, and what he did in each situation.

How did the Prophet treat his friends? What did he do at home? How was he with children? How did he eat, drink water? How did he perform his prayer (salah)? What did he pay attention to when talking, laughing, sleeping, walking, joking?

So we must learn these things and add his light to our own.

Well then, should I use a toothbrush or miswak?

A few weeks ago, I was having a conversation with a few of my dear friends. The subject went back and forth and came to the health of our mouth and teeth. We all knew how sensitive the Prophet was about the cleanliness of teeth and how he ordered us to look after them well. But there was this problem:

The Prophet used to clean his teeth with miswak. During that period, neither

toothpaste nor toothbrush existed. But they do today. You can also find dental floss, electrical toothbrushes and mouth wash. Apart from all these, there's also miswak.

So how should we, who are trying to be like the Prophet, trying to live like him, trying to make our lifestyle resemble his, clean our teeth?

With a toothbrush, or with miswak?

One of my friends said:

"Of course we should use a toothbrush! Miswak is out of date!"

Another protested:

"No never! Our Prophet used miswak! We should also use miswak!"

Another, probably because he was scared this argument would turn into a fight, said:

"It's best to use miswak-flavoured toothpaste!" In his own way, he had found a compromise.

We all couldn't help laughing at this answer!

You wonder what I said in that little argument with my friends.

I didn't say anything!

It was as if the lid on a jar full of ants was opened inside my head. And all those ants were spreading all over my brain.

I had to find an answer to this question and put those ants back in their jar. Otherwise, I was going to get a headache.

What should I do? Clean my teeth with miswak or toothbrush?

Which one would I have to do to go by the Prophet's sunnah?

That night, I asked myself a question:

"Why did our Prophet use miswak?"

This was an easy question:

"To clean his teeth of course!"

Then I drew a huge circle on a piece of paper and wrote 'The sunnah of cleaning teeth' on it.

Yes, taking care of cleaning mouth and teeth was one of the Prophet's sunnahs that he insisted on. He often warned his friends on this topic. He asked his ummah to keep their teeth clean.

When I'm cleaning my teeth with miswak, dental floss, toothpaste, or any other invention people may come up with in the future, if I remember and know that cleaning teeth are part of the Prophet's sunnah, I would be in that 'Clean teeth circle' and have carried out one of the Prophet's sunnahs that bring health and welfare to our lives. And Allah would (God willing) reward me for trying to be like the Prophet. I could very well earn the reward of sunnah by cleaning my teeth. Because our Prophet also cleaned his teeth.

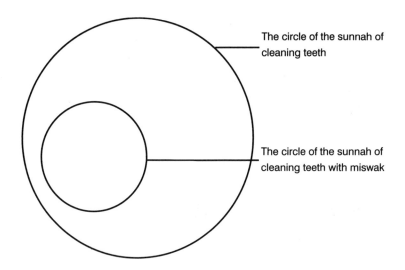

The circle of the sunnah of cleaning teeth

The circle of the sunnah of cleaning teeth with miswak

Well what would happen if I did this with miswak?

I drew another circle in the circle I had previously drawn and wrote 'The sunnah of cleaning teeth with miswak' on that.

If I clean my teeth with miswak, I would go into the circle with that acted as suited the Prophet's sunnah exactly, as they – like the Prophet – clean their teeth with miswak.

That night I made a decision! I was going to continue cleaning my teeth with toothbrush and toothpaste morning and night, as I had

been doing for years. Because cleaning my
teeth in this way was much easier for me.
When the Prophet had to make a decision
between two things – as long as it wasn't a sin
– he would choose the easier one! But as soon
as possible I was going to get myself a nice,
fresh and proper miswak as well. Because the
Prophet cleaned his teeth with miswak. He
also highly recommended his ummah to use
miswak.

About miswak

During the next few days, I started to wonder about miswak. As the Prophet had chosen it to clean his teeth, there must have been many reasons behind this.

Miswak was a plant that had been used by people for many centuries. It is made from the branches of a tree called arak or peelu. It is grown in hot areas reaching from east Africa to India.

In recent studies, it has been discovered that miswak had more benefits than could be found in any toothpaste and toothbrush put together.

Miswak, apart from just cleaning teeth, also strengthens gums.

Using miswak increases salivary juice, which prevents gums from drying up.

It also has a germ killing property.

As the fibres are made up of plant crystals their cleaning power is much greater and they are much more sensitive than toothbrushes.

These fibres, apart from cleaning the surface

of the teeth, can also go in between teeth like dental floss, to clean those areas as well.

The part of miswak that is used needs to be cut once a week and a new end needs to be opened.

In this way, it's like you use a new toothbrush every week! And without spending a penny more as well! Oh and by the way, there's no toothpaste cost either!

Apart from all these things, miswak is not something made from chemicals in a factory like toothpaste and toothbrush. It's a stick from one of Allah's trees. It's natural, pure, and non-polluting… This alone, is a good enough reason to choose miswak over toothbrush!

Let's not forget it is also a sunnah and the Prophet ordered people to clean their teeth with miswak 1400 years ago. He ordered it a lot as well. He used to say,

"Make it a habit to use miswak, as it is a means of cleansing the mouth and pleasing Allah".

– Ahmed

About the author

ÖZKAN ÖZE WAS born in Turkey in 1974. While at high school, he started working at Zafer magazine's editorial office in Istanbul and discovered his love of literature and books. Since then he has gone on to become the editor of Zafer Publications Group and continually writes. He is married with two children.

Özkan wrote the "I Wonder About Islam" series because he believes that questions are prayers. Asking one is like saying, "Teach me to understand." They act as keys that lead us through doors to new worlds that are more interesting and beautiful than we thought possible.

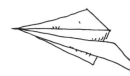

The "I Wonder About Islam" series

The "I Wonder About Islam" series give young readers answers to the BIG questions they have about Islam in brilliant little books. Written in a friendly and accessible style for today's youth, these are essential companions for questioning young minds.

Books in the "I Wonder About Islam" series:

I Wonder About Allah (Book One)

I Wonder About Allah (Book Two)

I Wonder About the Prophet (Book Three)

I Wonder About the Qur'an (Book Four)

I Wonder About Heaven (Book Five)

I Wonder About Fate (Book Six)

I Wonder About Angels (Book Seven)